Hunter Johnson Presents...

THE NEWS

1

FOREWORD
By Terrence Brown

Years ago, a very close friend of mine asked a question. We were surrounded by two or three of our mutual companions. At first, no one understood the question and even I had to pause. He asked a very simple, but complex question. In a serious and inquisitive tone, he stated, "What is sight without vision?" I am positive that everyone except my close friend was thinking "What in the world are we talking about here". However, I soon realized the essence of the question and the essence of the man asking the question. Willie Jerome Johnson Jr. aka "Hunter" was the man who posed that question to us years ago. Thru the years, Hunter posed that question to many people and a majority of the people got the essence of the question. However, everyone did not care about answering it. To them, it was just Hunter being Hunter. To me, it was Hunter striving for answers to the never ending dilemmas of life. Being from a small country town, residents are conditioned to the story of failure and not success. The ratio of failure to success in our hometown is 5-1 and the measuring stick is not based off of money or other material things. It is based on doing the right thing and striving to become a better person each day. Although success is an intangible goal and there are many differing opinions, Hunter is the epitome of success. Many of you may ask the question, "Why give such a label?" The only way to answer that question is to pose another question, "What is sight without vision?"

Thanks to Willie J. Johnson and his lovely wife Kemiya Johnson for this once in a lifetime opportunity. It truly is an honor to be a part of this book and an honor to call them true friends. So readers enjoy the _News_ and expand the vision of life!

Today

Between attempts at escapades, for a willing ear, I need a lender,

So I sit down and order a drink, and proceed to converse with the bartender.

She tells me she was glad that I sat down, she'd always wanted to talk to me,

But I, usually, was talking to some lady, she didn't want to interrupt my speech.

"Well, you've got me here, right now, and have my undivided attention,

Anything you've ever wanted to say, now's as good a time as any to mention."

"I've always wanted to know who you are, from likes and dislikes to where you're from,

And what it is you tell the girls, 'cause there's always a pretty lady on your arm."

I laugh, at first, when she says that, nothing but smiles riddle my face,

I am impressed that she knew what she wanted, elated she's cutting to the chase.

I try to explain exactly what it is, but speechlessness prompts my hesitation,

I guess my insatiable love for women, has been my only explanation.

"It isn't a massive love for lust, that fuels my constant exploring,

But sincere need to satisfy women's wants, that is motivation to my alleged whoring.

Has it all been sexual relations, sweet words, pancakes, and back rubs,

Not even, sometimes, mere conversation, a feeling like they are needed and loved."

I see, in her face, there is interest, compelled by the tale I am telling,

Without trying, I can see what is happening, my words, again, are prevailing.

I continue along with my message, probing deeply into my paradigm,

"There's no secret to my success in dating, ladies seem to hang on to my written lines."

Her expression says she is part confused, seems as though I say something outta sight,

It makes sense when I said speech's, sometimes, amiss, so I find it easier just to write.

"Emails written randomly, in the height of the day, to see how their day may be going,

Or sending texts in a crowded room, complimenting for the sake of her knowing."

So much for ms. bartender, fresh out the barber's chair, nice clothes—I feel kinda fly,

Now, over the rim of my cognac glass, a girl on the dance floor, has caught my eye.

She's moving so free to the music, her body is so delighting,

As the dimmed light flickers on her smooth silhouette, her form is oh so inviting.

My movements are calculated, I give her the show that she has given to me,

She seems to hang on to my every word, from when I first part my lips to speak.

I pride myself on being a southern gent, and I am sure that she's taking notice,

Not once from her eyes to her heaving cleavage, has my attention shifted its focus.

For more intimacy, we sit at a booth, so we can speak more calm and talk more clear,

I want her undivided attention, to drop a little bug in her ear.

Around the block twice or thrice, sure, so I'm a worldly renaissance man,

She confides in me, she rarely talks to her guy, but with me, she sees that she can.

We chat for what seems a minute, but we cover quite a lot,

She's managed to tell me everything she wants, and everything that her man is not.

She says she wants to leave, at once, but if I'd like, then, we can just stay,

We won't need a cab to her place, she only lives a few blocks away.

We're at her apartment in a minute, one thing standing between me and her becoming us,

Is the small formality of the keys, and getting the lock to open up fast enough.

I am ready to be mannish, as she locks the door, and I am not trying to play nice,

But I think it might be in our best interest, if I impart a word of advice.

"Nobody better get mad, or pay visits, because you tried to holler,

Like the men of internet age, I've got my own kind of pop-up blocker."

And with that being said, once again, her heavy chest started heaving,

We, now, excuse ourselves to the back, and have ourselves a wonderful evening.

Joe D. bid his date farewell, when dressed, he reached for his shoes and keys,

An eventful evening with his latest tryst—easy release left his heart at ease.

She walked him to the door, he slid his jacket on his shoulders,

Cloaking joy, he could've whistled "Dixie," from the way she worked him over.

Always the consummate gentleman, no one ever has to remind him,

Just as he does, each and every time, he allowed her time to lock the door behind him.

Exhausted but had no plans to stay, he'd go home and hit the sack,

Rest assured he was on his way, when he heard the deadbolt hit the latch.

On his way to the stairs, he found himself entranced, his heart consumed,

From a door cracked down the hall, a light glimmering over a shadow in the room.

Curiosity seemed to draw him in, the direction of the outward facing knob,

The mood seemed so somber, sniffles signaled excruciating sobs.

Not the safest of neighborhoods, so who'd leave the door open behind them,

Unless, of course, it was on purpose, and they'd meant for someone to find them.

He reasoned with himself if, in fact, he should just mind his business,

It seemed as if a greater power, guided him to proceed to pay a visit.

Anita said to herself, My heart has grown so heavy and broken, it's a sin,

What if I were to slit my wrist, and let some air come in?

Since the pleas of my soul, haven't dried the ducts of my eyes,

Maybe a subtle suicide, will calm the cries of my tries.

I give all I have, and all that comes to me is this,

Sorrow in my life, while they tear my heart to pieces.

Will anyone care, if I hit a tree at full throttle,

Or if I take pill after pill, until I see the bottom of the bottle?

What will the world lose, I am nothing special to look at,

I'm sure the men can find another to diss, they can get another doormat.

I go to church on Sundays, do right to strangers and loved ones,

All I want, in return, is affection from a loving husband.

Just as Anita is about, to carry out her chosen fate,

There comes a knock at her door, thank the Lord, it isn't too late.

"I know this might sound kind of lame, but I promise it's not a lie,

I was passing in the hall and heard a sob, and can't stand to hear ladies cry."

Anita looks into Joe D.'s eyes and, immediately, feels he isn't lying,

That he'd really merely been passing by, and stopped as he heard her crying.

"Sir, I really appreciate your concern, but I'm digressing from a chosen job,

So, please, excuse me," *she manages to get out, between her cries and sobs.*

He shrugs and turns to vacate the home, right back through the same door post,

But it seems that something is nudging him, and saying she doesn't want him to go.

Joe tries to oblige, and let her come to lock the door,

When, through his wandering eyes, he sees a sleeping pill bottle on the floor.

"Ma'am, I don't mean to be nosy, because, my business, this really isn't,

But I hope you aren't preparing, to go and make a rash decision."

Her hands tremble as, from a cigarette, she pulls and takes a drag,

Then, she empties out the contents, of her lipstick-stained liquor glass.

"Mister, I'm not sure just who you are, and what brings you to me,

But, for so long, I have been bound down, and just want, now, to be free."

"My name is Joe D., and I was headed from a friend's place from visitation,

So, to me, finding you here and now, fate serves to be the only explanation."

"I can't make the pain disappear, I'm no miracle or magician,

But if you want someone to talk to, I am more than willing to listen.

At least give yourself that much time, before you decide to fade to black,

Because, once you travel down that road, there will be no coming back."

She introduces herself as Anita Mann, and lifts her weeping eyes to the sky,

Because, despite her despair and cry for help, she doesn't really want to die.

Joe knows there is no part, that he can afford to ignore,

So he pays close attention, while Anita tells him her story.

"Each time I give my heart to someone, and they break my heart in two,

I have my liberation planned out in my mind, have it figured out what I'm going to do.

I pack my things and turn to leave, get my "Dear John" letter ready,

Then, they speak the sweetest words to me, and always seem to get me."

"My mind's made up, I've had enough, and then, all of a sudden,

Like playing a video game console, it's like I hit the "reset button."

All the pain is about to go, I'm finally done, or so it seems,

Then, I fall for the false hope they sell, and I'm back in the recurring dream."

"Each bad thing they've done, is erased by each and every kind word they've said,

And the problem only compounds if, by chance, I gap open my legs.

The troubles I encounter, would not seem so hard for me to solve them,

If, only, I would go ahead and move forward, instead of always resetting my problems."

Meanwhile, somewhere across town, through all the cross streets and the bi-ways,

There's a young man taking his own life away, but chooses to do it the high way.

He burns every tree and herb, that could be found in a field,

His dependence has become so potent, people, now, call him Chief Sitting Still.

Though he may not be an Indian, he definitely has his reservations,

Of getting in the swing of life, and embracing it's natural matriculation.

Not a Native, but American, he lives life in a daze,

He finds himself in stalking white rows, his shambled life is just a maze.

He may roll or hit the pipe, it's doubtful if he smokes to secure his peace,

More likely, it is for his own leisure, or for his own mind's release.

Chilling and hanging the day away, traveling the world backward, around the clock,

Talking and walking the streets, all day long, doing his best to hold down the block.

He shows no intrinsic value, the world regards him as being worthless,

It seems there is no inner drive to him, no sense of passionate purpose.

He lives life as it comes, with him, there is no forward focus,

There is one thing he's romantic about, and that's the idea of being hopeless.

Not a nice word to say, not a thought to provoke,

Not a quiet prayer to pray, he's regarded as nothing but a joke.

Protected by his rep, he never stands alone to fight,

Now, he's robbing, stealing, cheating, even rumored snorting white.

Heating, steady heating, everything he speaks is just for show,

Breathing, barely breathing, tries to play the part of loco.

Heeding, so deceiving, should speak true words, but no, no,

He calls himself a gangster, but is far from a mafioso.

Trendy fads like the grill he licks, are all means of getting chicks,

Guess satisfaction won't come until, he trades the pills and hits for busting bricks.

Cutting slices of rocks, as white as alabaster,

It would be better to be a mastermind, than for him to mind his master.

His work's been slow, while whipping rock from blow, like he'll usually do,

No goods to sell, no lawns to mow, the recession's hit the crackheads, too.

Though no clientele for the dope he sells, his habit's calling so money's a hurdle,

So he makes up in his mind, tonight, he's going to go and be a burglar.

Phil wipes his feet on the worn welcome mat, and wipes sweat from his eyelids,

Shuts the door behind him, gently—careful not to wake the wife and kids.

Washes up in the small face bowl, picks the cotton from his hair,

Says his grace over the humble meal, that his wife left, for him, prepared.

Finishes with his dinner plate, and turns off all of the lights,

Kneels to say his nightly prayers, and kisses his kids goodnight.

Just as ol' Phil Myhand, starts dozing off to sleep,

He's startled from subtle slumber, when the door begins to creak.

Paternal instincts kick in, though he is sure he turned the lock,

He grabs the pistol from the nightstand drawer, planning protection at any cost.

He knows his house in and out, in twenty years of marriage, he's had none other,

Easing to the kitchen table, unheard, he puts the gun's barrel to the head of a burglar.

"My thirty-eight's to your head, and its nose is a snub,

You make one false move, and I'll paint these walls with your blood.

Why are you in my house, I ain't got nothing for you to steal,

I'm a man trying to feed my family, in earnest, and I been fired from the mill."

"I'll only ask once if you got a gun, it's the middle of the night and you're trying to loot,

Tell the truth, 'cause I'd be right, in the eyes of the law, if I decide I'm going to shoot."

The man, with hands raised high, begins to speak, through the gold teeth in his grill,

"Don't shoot me, old man, I don't have a gun, and folks call me Chief Sitting Still."

"I don't know why you think you can go around, robbing and thieving and stealing,

Have you ever thought that folks you're stealing from, go to work and work for a living?"

"Old man, I promise I'll do anything, I hope like hell that you hear me,

You name it, and I'll make it happen, long as you let me live and don't up and kill me."

"The first thing you can do is uncover your head, and then, you can watch your mouth,

I might not kill you, but this is for sure, you will not, again, disrespect my house."

With a left-handed grip, Phil held the trigger, and dared Chief to as much as sneeze,

Reaching with the right to the phone on the wall, he didn't hesitate to call the police.

"Sit at the table with your hands on top, the man's on his way—no sudden moves, you,
If you try anything funny before they get here, 'fore God in Heaven, I'll surely shoot you.
Lawd have mercy, the devil's really busy, everywhere you turn there's another ditch,
We all got problems, but none worth freedom, what, son, has brought you to this?"

There, Chief's best option may really be, to do as Phil Myhand insisted,
But storms are brewing all around the city, from the heights to the Red Light District.
Heat lightning's lighting the night's sky, but the neon lamps burn in everyone's eyes,
Kimmie Samoa cares less about the present weather, she just wants more things to buy.

The mall is cool for certain things, but boutiques, I often crowd them,
Cheap knockoffs in swap meets and markets, I can really do without them.
If you want to watch me get hot, then, buy me some Versace,
Only Prada and Louis V., really do something to get through to me.

All I'm saying I want is, security in my life,
The average Joe can have a chance, once he gets his money right.
When I make my decisions in love, I am trying to win,
I have been dead broke, before, and refuse to be, again.

Sometime, broke jokers get it misconstrued, wanting my number, so they can call me,

But they do need to understand, that I am a high-dollar dolly.

I'm all about my paper, a diva, well in-tune with the shot calling,

And will not waste my time, unless big rims or nice clothes insinuate you're balling.

Some people say men won't buy the cow, when they can get the milk for free,

All of the people that feel this way, must have been referring to me.

See, I've never been a rancher, and could care less about a cow,

But if it is money that you want to get, I can, surely, tell you how.

I enjoy the finer things, in life, but I'm not mistaken for a workaholic,

And if, by chance, I find true love, it'll be at the bottom of a rich man's wallet.

I wish critics would reconsider, before they say that I'm a gold digger,

What they should simply understand, is my beauty is just not for the lowest bidder.

Take for instance my old man, he's old enough to be my daddy,

He depends on his Viagra, but his money lets him have me.

Right now, he's out doing what he does, probably chasing a young piece of coochie,

But he takes me shopping when I say so, so you know that I am Gucci.

What do you know, Kimmie Samoa is right, and while she is spending money shopping,

Her old man is out on the town, as always, and longing to see some panties dropping.

What does it matter, to him, her tab, or how much money she blows and spends,

He's wealthy and never misses money, so doesn't need to count dollars and cents.

I'm on the town, most every night; I've grown accustomed to the stares,

Every time I leave my house, I dress with such great style and flare.

The women all stand in line, not now, like they once did,

Hair dye masquerades my age, but I like to live my life like a kid.

I always hear the last call for alcohol; I visit places 'til the lights come on,

My joy is found in the bars and cars, because I have no family at home.

Pretty groupies, every night, find such delight, in trying to get me in their britches,

I know their love for me is superficial, they just want to stake claim to my riches.

It's cool, though, matters not to me, who cares about their motivation,

I give them what they give to me, no need to remember their names or occupations.

My name's Asa Plenty, name speaks for itself, in the industry I chose, I thrived,

I lost my kid and wife in a single death, but I'm here, so that means I survived.

Trophies on my arm, clothes in the closet, choice of any car I choose to crank,

I drink the finest liquor, spend how I want, there's dollars I never knew I had in the bank.

Man of the community, I think I'll pass, let the squares deal with that fad,

Who wouldn't want the life that I live, I can't say my life is too bad.

Asa seems as though he loves his life, he has an abundance of money to blow,

The life he's lived since a young man, many unfortunates may never know.

But what a small world, on the very streets that he frequents and is currently roaming,

Life's not so pleasant for Misty Goodlife—spending her night moaning and groaning.

For my love, he would have stood convicted, with no hope for an acquittal,

Willing to kill the biggest rock, and put a brick into the hospital.

Never chose to call me names, refrained from the harshest things he wanted to say,

Nor did he ever indulge in all the games, that men his age may tend to play.

What is meant by "fiasco," define what it means to "blow it,"

Imagine having what I've wanted all of my life, I'm the reason I lost it and I know it.

Distancing myself from advances, compiling his feelings of my hurt,

Holding too strong to my stances, wanting him to conform to standards that I set forth.

Appreciation for the life that I once had, arrogance helped me, seldom, to show it,

In fact, it is my foolish pride, regarding my perfect man, that had ensured that I blow it.

For what most of the world would ogle over and, likely, deem romance,

And of what most of the world's young girls dream, I messed over and blew my chance.

My lips, now, tremble like piano strings, my eyes are running faucets,

I wish I had places to hide my head, would be better off hiding out in the closet.

With each passing moment, I grow more lonely, and my hunger grows much stronger,

Holding nothing but memories to keep me sane, and my pillow is left to comfort.

Some people like to call me, the name "night stalker,"

I prefer to be referred to, by the term "street walker."

I am unhappy in the things I'm doing, I have compounded pain,

Reminiscent of the life I was pursuing, before I flushed it down the drain.

Something straight from a fairy tale, Prince Charming was the man I had,

But I shunned his white unicorn, and treated him pretty bad.

Now, my furniture smells of nicotine, my clothes are laced with scents of marijuana,

I never receive quality time, because my man's always out on the corner.

I guess what a person has, depends on what he or she chooses,

I traded being held and spooning, for my current black and blue bruises.

I should be on my knees, praying to my God, to deliver me from this,

Instead of on my knees, in these parking lots, or in motel rooms turning tricks.

Small world, maybe, but in big cities, it's rare that you find,

People with very little in common, finding their paths intertwined.

Asa Plenty's made it clear and plain, from his evening, the things he would like,

And as fate would have it, if he is lucky, he may get it from voluptuous Misty Goodlife.

At my usual Saturday hangout, I see a lady from afar,

She takes a pull of her cigarette, as she sits, alone, at the bar.

Pretty like I like 'em, and she has the nicest ass,

My plan is to wine and dine this chick, but skimp her on the cash.

Definition of a mack, I am the original playboy bunny,

I have all of the honeys, because I have all of the money.

I approach and offer to buy a drink, maybe we can drink the night away,

'Cause I know Courvoisier might make you say, what everyday talk just don't display.

She says, "My money is kinda funny, and my change is a little strange,

But the rent man don't care nothing bout it, and the light bill still remains.

My man is a dead beat, and that's a fact, but my baby still needs feeding,

I'm trying to make a little cash, do you need some company for the evening?"

I am struck by the fact she is blunt and such, though, it still turns me on,

In a matter of a couple brief moments, I have the girl and I am gone.

No need to exercise my gift for lies, no need to extend my game,

Moments later, we check into a cheap motel, where all the staff knows me by name.

I have been around the block a few times, but don't enjoy this as much as I ought to,

This young girl is just a desperate mother and, too, she is somebody's daughter.

She excuses herself to the bathroom, to freshen up and to get herself ready,

I leave my card and cash on the dresser, anything else, my conscience wouldn't let me.

It seems that Asa has an outer body experience, as he hurriedly turns and walks away,

And as a surprise to even himself, he begins to part his lips and pray.

"Lord, it's been a while since we've talked, but I don't know how much I can stand,

That girl I met, tonight, made me see, I've been the worst kind of man."

"Wallowing in a cess pool of sin, is the only honest reason,

I haven't been to Your house, in a whole lot of pecan seasons.

When Mama took me to church, as a boy, they said no man knows the day nor the hour,

You answered my prayers of riches, and I let that mean that You gave me power."

"I have been running for so long and, now, I have no hiding places left,

I am being tried by a test of fire, in denial and not even honest with myself.

I haven't felt conviction, since I've been of drinking age,

And have vexed and sexed scores of hookers, like a convict freed from his cage."

"But, tonight, I felt a shrieking pain, toward that young girl after I had chose her,

The pain hit my heart and spine and, then, the chill began to spread all over.

I don't know who she is, Lord, perhaps, I've seen her once or twice,

But something just wouldn't let me help, add further detriment to her life."

Asa quickly turns the corner, hoping to catch a taxi to drive him home,

So he can sit and reflect, alone, but is startled by his ringing phone.

When he answers the caller's call, he hears car horns and other familiar sounds,

The caller's heavily breathing voice—heels beating the pavement in the background.

"I was hoping I would catch you, on my way back to the spot,

I couldn't chance finding you another night, my face you'd have soon forgot.

I probably shouldn't question this, looking a gift horse in the mouth,

Instead, pocketing your crispy bills, to put some groceries in my house."

"I, once, was a beauty queen, I have been the cock of the walk,

But, now, I'm a shadow of myself, walking for cock around the clock holds my stock.

This is of no consequence to you, I'm a face, to you, with no name,

But you left the money on the dresser, so I want to please you, just the same."

"Pride from persons in my position, may come across surprising,

But, sir, let me assure you, that, truly, I am not lying.

Though, I do appreciate the gift you gave, please don't think that I don't,

It's just rare in my line of work, so please come to the room and tell me what you want."

The guilt he had felt, just moments ago, seems to have vanished and his burden fell,

So, he agrees to turn around, and meet the beautiful young lady back at the motel.

By the time he arrives, he has had a vision, wiping away his pending sadness,

He thinks he's sure where he knows her from, and it leads him to feel gladness.

Asa had felt an eerie feeling, he was unable to, as he'd usually, use her,

He kept feeling she seemed familiar, and like he already knew her.

She opens up the door, with a sharply piercing glance,

Her fine frame enhanced, when her shaved legs lock out in a thoroughbred stance.

Her dress fits like a glove—makeup and lips painted blood red help to disguise her,

It is when he looks in eyes that can't lie, that he realizes from where he recognizes her.

"There are two things that I want, in fact, the first is just to talk,

The next, I will address, later, if you choose to stay instead of up and walk."

"Tell me all about yourself, I'm interested to know all about you,

The only way my deal will stick, is if you tell me the complete truth.

Young lady, do not understand me wrong, I'm no freak with plans to stalk you,

Just an old man who, once, was young, and, now, needs someone to talk to."

"I want to know of your family life, tell me what motivates you,

Let me know why you choose the life, that constantly depreciates you.

I know what I ask is a hard request, and it may prove quite tough to,

Spill your soul to a stranger, who could possibly judge you."

"Trust, I'm in no position to judge; I'm sure my story's worse,

My second request will make more sense, after you have fulfilled the first."

A stickler for customer service, she takes his request and consents,

Then, they take a seat at the foot of the bed in the motel room he had previously rented.

Yesterday

Misty was skeptical—this was, certainly, an unusual request and she'd never forget it,

She had never had a john want to hear her story, but she burned, inside, to tell it.

As she sat next to Asa, on the bed, it's as if her entire demeanor changed,

A lady in control, to a vulnerable girl confiding in a man who didn't know her name.

"My reason needs repairing; for my choices, I truly need my bottom beat,

I once had it all, but now climb poles at these shows, in order to get my ends to meet.

I had a man who never chose to mistreat me, never had a need to hit me or holler,

Now, I check integrity and pride at the door, compromising my morals for dollars."

"A relationship so perfect, he was such a gentleman, always managed to bring me joy,

What did I do to show my gratitude, cheated on him with a low down dope boy.

I took his kindness for weakness, ran over him—tried to use him to carry out my will,

Then, I cheated on my beloved Joe D., for my new deadbeat Chief Sitting Still."

"I, Misty Goodlife, find it so hard to find a man, who is not just after my draws,

That makes my decision to have left Joe D. so hard, he accepted me, in spite of my flaws.

I could have been a better girl, to give him myself, fully, I always had my reservation,

Now, I have to live with my decision, if I could change it, I would with no hesitation."

Asa's eyes were blood-shot red, his tear ducts strained from holding back his tears,

He just rubbed his hands together, as he shook his head, thinking of his own years.

He gave her a silk handkerchief, to wipe her tears as they started pouring,

He empathized with her pain, and tried to cheer her by telling her his story.

"Misty, like I'm arrested, I'm stressed and I'm restless,

I've rested my nest egg, in these worthless investments.

I wore Armani on my back, and alligators on my feet,

Sporting wood-framed Cartiers, I had Egyptian cotton sheets."

"I was careful when it came to scandal, my money helped me to prevent it,

I had private physicians on my payroll, so I'd never have to visit a clinic.

Any habit women had, if they'd give me pleasure, I would fund it,

Imagine how long I did it, I've had money since there were small heads on the hundreds."

"I used to move in Judy, and romance with Nancy,

Suzy usually blew me, I lived in the pants of Angie.

Having all the best threads and shoes, with the ladies, gave me all the luck,

What good is it to me, now, women are gone, and clothes are only collecting dust."

"I put so much time and money in cars and broads, lived life like I'd never done,
Put no effort into making my marriage work, did bare minimum in raising my son.
I spend days and nights paying for companionship and, still, am so all alone,
So much time spent in these hotel rooms, no one would believe that I have a home."

"The mess that I chose to make of my life, still proved not be enough for me,
I guess it's like the old saying goes, misery really does love having company.
I made the decisions, so I'm the one that blew the hand I was dealt, for certain,
As if that weren't enough, there was an upright man; I made it my business to hurt him."

"Ol' Phil Myhand was a heck of a man, he was always the last to complain,
Schooled by hard knocks, his best release, was whistlin' to ease his pain.
Co-workers found his sound soothing, no one waited on quittin' time for dismissal,
But all would fight for a spot next to Phil eating lunch, for a chance to hear him whistle."

"Phil had lived for all of his years, living deep in the country,
His opportunities were few, and his pockets had even less money.
It was hard for him to read or write, or even to explain himself,
But he found the greatest joy, when he whistled to entertain himself."

"And whistle, he did, for grown folks and kids, his tune could ease any hurt,

He could, sometimes, rouse the spirit, all around could feel it, like a pipe organ at church.

His reliable renditions were the absolute best, and no one could deny,

That, even in the most trying times, he could raise your spirits high."

"The sound was strong and pure and, yet, as delicate as a feather,

The ups and downs, of the melody, were so precise and well put together.

Notes kneaded so neatly, even soulful singers could not bash him,

With a tone that was so strong and long, even yellow canaries couldn't match them."

"Though he proved to be one hell of a man, I can't say I was the one who hired him,

But, now, it is with the greatest regret, that I have to admit I was the one who fired him.

He was so loved at home and at work, the workers missed him when he was not there,

I had so much when he had so little and, yet, what he had was too much for me to bear."

As Asa and Misty sat, shared their plights in life, and cried,

Joe D. still talked with Anita, in the apartment that she almost died.

Undoubtedly, she had made him think of the effect he may be having on his trysts,

Affecting them, as she had been, so he explained what had helped make him who he is.

"I could not seem to keep my food down, the idea, alone, was somewhat hideous,

I had been faithful to my lovely girlfriend, so it was only she that gave me Chlamydia.

I had her on my mind, every night and day—visualized how to give her a ring,

I was shocked when I went to use the bathroom, and noticed my private did sting."

"I went to the clinic to check it out, and asked the doctor what were the odds,

He said that the best advice he could give, was to think, twice, before doing it raw.

By that time, I was beside myself, I was shaking with all the mounting anger,

How could she be so inconsiderate, putting my life in such imminent danger?"

"How could she do that, who was it that she would cheat with,

My thoughts began to curse her name, my mind filled to the rim with expletives.

Since that day, I've changed my ways, in my dealings with female friends,

The encounter didn't harden my heart, it just won't happen ever again."

Joe was able to bring Anita some comfort; He was able to raise her spirits, some,

By letting her know that, though sad, not only ladies go down the road she'd gone.

Though his testimony, had calmed the flames of her pain and help get her stable,

Fireworks were just beginning for Chief Sitting Still, at Phil Myhand's kitchen table.

"What all you wanna know, old man, is this supposed to make me legit,

But, just the same, I'll talk to you, what you see is what you get.

You think I enjoy causing pain, my mother died when I was ten,

My pops provided, financially, but he never was a friend."

"It seemed he could hardly wait, 'til he'd no longer have to feed me,

As soon as I came of age, he didn't hesitate to cut me off, completely.

Not that he was really ever there, he spent time and money in strip clubs with dancers,

My mother coped by smoking and, as a result, died after a bout with cancer."

"I lived in his home with him hardly there—he only made sure that I could eat,

Searching for true family, of course, I had to turn to the streets.

Hustlers and gangbangers, served as surrogate uncles and brothers,

It's a shame I sacrificed my girl to them, because I think I really loved her."

"It was not just Anita's heart I broke, when I shared the love of her father's daughter,

But mine, too, when she gave me Chlamydia, after I gave her to my partners.

How dumb could I be, losing the best blessing that I had ever known,

And picking up chain smoking, traveling down the same road my mother had gone."

"Her smokes of choice were cigarettes, and I had chosen reefer,

From recreational to daily, I grew into a "chiefer."

My name came from my habit, to support it, I make do,

By doing what I'm doing, and it is that that's brought me, here, to you. "

Tomorrow

Before Chief finished his monologue, he was interrupted by a siren,

Short and sweet, it just gave one beep, blue lights twirled and flashed like lightning.

Phil Myhand lowered his gun, when he realized he had back up,

He wiped his eyes, as he let the cops in, thinking of the young man's bad luck.

He didn't put up the slightest fight, just fully expecting the police would rough him,

After wiping his eyes, he bowed his head, positioning his hands so they could cuff him.

The older gentleman lifted his head, as he addressed the sergeant,

"I apologize for wasting your time, because I won't be pressing charges."

"He's been terrorizing the city streets, with any and everything corrupt,

Now, you are telling me, you won't lock this bastard up?"

"He tried to burglarize my house, so it is my right to choose,

So, if you would be so kind, I'd appreciate if you'd let him loose."

"Let me say it this way, sir, should this happen in the future,

I can't guarantee, the response time will be so quick, and we'll get the intruder."

"Mr. Officer, if a robber threatens to come harm me or my family,

I reckon, if you all don't come, my old pistol will just have to handle it."

"I clearly understand your warnings, trust, fully, I will be heeding,

But it is quite late, so, now, it's time you boys be leaving."

Seeing that Phil wouldn't budge, the sergeant keyed the cuff hole and turned the key,

Then, Phil watched the chains that bound Chief's hands fall, as he was set free.

Phil stood on the front porch, and watched the cops' lights 'til they drove out of sight,

Wisdom told him that though Chief was free, if he left, it would be a long night.

"They'll never let it rest like that; you'll be cornered wherever you're going,

If you leave, now, you'll be dead or in jail for strike three, by in the morning."

With a look of confusion, before Chief could speak his statement,

He admired how the man he'd tried to rob, spoke like an elder statesman.

"I just tried to burglarize your house, so I know you're not a fan,

What's it to you, anyway, what do you care, old man?"

He probably shouldn't, but Chief pressed the issue, becoming more persistent,

Phil shook his head at Chief's ignorance trying, himself, not to become indignant.

"Son, open your eyes, for a minute, and tell me what you see,

Of course, we aren't exactly alike but, son, still, you look just like me."

"I'm closer to my three scores and ten, sooner than you, I'll be carried in a coffin,

I chose to spare one life, tonight, but that won't solve our entire problem.

How many do you think are out, tonight, doing just what you were trying to do,

And out of those, how many will be spared, like God led me to spare you?"

Chief's lip quivered as he spoke to Phil Myhand, "What you're saying is I am blessed,"

Because you felt, in your heart, I was fit to live, I might not be so lucky the next."

Okay, what needs to happen, how can you help my generation to get,

Out of the rut I'm in, and not make decisions so stupid?"

With glimmers of hope in his eyes, puffed up by wrinkles of the years,

He pulled two chairs close together, as he fought away the tears.

"I'm going to tell you what needs to happen, exactly what you need to do,

You are the next generation of our community, it ends and starts with you."

"No matter what people think they know or may, often, tend to believe,

I say you're never too long in the tooth, for demons to be released.

The image you display, won't always prove to take you farthest,

I've seen life whip the biggest man, and succeed to destroy the hardest."

"Life's roadmaps will, sometimes, have their imperfections,

There are times when you have to take steps back, to get pointed in the right direction.

Forge forward and be not, you, discouraged,

Steel your will, hold your head, and drink a glass of courage."

"This advice might help you choose sensible choices, to sneak past perdition,

Relieve a guilty conscience, amidst the lingering suspicion.

Retire from being a pimp, and tell your girl, so she can know,

There's more to life than being a whore, selling ass from door to door."

"Keep your temper to yourself, leave domestic violence alone,

Never be willing to sacrifice your freedom, trying to re-raise somebody grown.

Don't think that spouting out kids, will make you a man or, simply, amazes,

It'll be hard for you to try to live, with them garnishing your wages."

"Examine the situation, to allow for better precision,

Don't lean so much on impulse, when making lasting decisions.

You are young enough to get education; your knowledge, you can't negate,

You can't make an offer they can't refuse, with one you can't articulate."

"So leave Daddy's pistol in the drawer, let Grandma keep her worn out stockings,

But keep the gears of your mind, well-oiled and away from locking.

Dig deep within your mind, so you can find your buried treasure,

Your current profession is temporary, and it cannot last forever."

As they continued their chat, Chief broke into tears, hugging Phil like a son would,

He vowed, from then on, he would point out bad and make all attempts to do good.

"Thank you, old man—I mean, Mr. Myhand, I don't know how to repay you."

"Son, just know I'm here to help you and thank God; He is the one who has saved you."

"Imagine what we've seen, tonight, witnesses to a miracle in the making,

A testimony to anyone who still needs proof, salvation is ours for the taking.

Do you think it is a coincidence, the way the scene played out,

With options of death or a stint in jail, you were provided with a way out."

"As if the whirling lights, like the lightening, weren't a sign of imminent capture,

The thunderous rap that followed, on the door, signified the end like the rapture.

It was the spirit of God that made a way; though, you did not see His face,

Like the Israelites, He let you see trouble so you could experience His grace."

"Everything happens in a season for a reason,

You've overcome to testify, and keep others like you from grieving.

You won't glorify the Lord, by what you preach and how you speak,

But you'll help to spread His kingdom, by your actions and your deeds."

Phil wasn't the only one aiming to help better a future, from wisdom of experience,

Joe D. had talked Anita out of suicide, and was convincing her of worth and benefit.

"Raise your eyes and lift your tilted head, do not keep it bowed down,

It will benefit no one, unless you fit it to bear a crown."

"So jolly from the fact, that you say that you are living single,

I feel like I want to dance, like I hear a toe-tapping jingle.

I'll try to provide some answers, if you'll stop crying like a baby,

I'll inform you of what most men want, and transform you into a lady."

"Give up what you think you know, put your search party down,

Your heart is full of good; it's just that you need to be found.

There's a certain set of things that I do know, you're as good a person as any to confide,

I'm going to save you from finding a man, and help you to be found as a bride."

"Women often inquire on the things, that men want most, sometimes,

So here is advice to tell your friends, and these things will not cost a dime.

All men want a girl they can treat like their lady, but play around with like a friend,

Can talk with the best, keep respect—girlie, kinda worldly, sexy every now and then."

"Take the time to shave your legs; don't let them grow wooly and bushy,

Invest in what will keep your Secret, and stay away from the Tussy.

Take an extra second, fresh out of the shower, to moisturize,

No one likes to hold chapped hands, or have to kiss on ashy thighs."

"As far as choosing a man, let's take it slow, I'll relate this analogy to one fishing,

Anytime you cast out your line, the bait is a big part of the fish you are getting.

If you often walk around exposed, no clothes, showing your body because it's a hot one,

That bait attracts a certain kind of fish, usually, a scavenger that feeds from the bottom."

"Whenever you meet new men, you always come across to them so nervous,

Like a commercial or newspaper ad, you try to sell your worth and your service.

Bullies often pick on the weakest ones, or the ones that they see as most conquerable,

When you come across as timid and shy, those things may make you seem vulnerable."

"Words from your mouth are like feathers in wind, released from a big pillow sack,

Once you let them out of your mouth, there is no way to take them back.

So if profane words mean disrespect, or you think that they will offend you,

Don't use them, because like Miranda Rights, your words can be used against you."

"Always be an equal, not superior or inferior; remember, you are not his daughter,

In actions and speech, always demand respect, that would be given from your father.

No calling out of names, or inflicting any pain, make that man have to put you first,

'Cause no matter what I tell you, it never will matter, until you are aware of your worth."

"Realize, relationships cannot be one-sided, they are partnerships, of sorts,

Just like you need to feel secure, he needs a cheerleader for support.

Old school tools, I'm sure he can use, yard work, opening doors and kissing hands,

Become friends with the pots and pans, if he takes on the old school jobs of the man."

"I have had enough women, had opportunity to learn and know,

That many choose to saturate their minds, with dog and pony shows.

If you took a survey, few of them could try to deny,

That, instead of the ugly truth, they'd rather have a pretty lie."

"They focus on their wishful wants, fairy tale lands all filled with glee,

Rather than living in reality, they build life on what they would have it to be.

Accepting kids and wives and double lives, things that are prearranged,

And promises of difficult things, which may be hard to re-arrange."

"Accepting number two, they make allowances to explain it,

Truth is if you're not the leading dog, the view never really changes.

Realize that hidden beauty, often times, is in the frog,

Be specific and prolific, and the tail can't wag the dog."

Anita thanked Joe D.—her crying transformed to giggles and smiles,

And true to his charismatic nature, he wooed and complimented her all the while.

"When I came here, last night, you were ready to throw in the towel—you were through,

Now, look at this polished diamond shine—just look at what God can do."

Not only did she thank him, in return, he promised to call when he got home,

He said that, because of her, he realized he needed to confront his past to move on.

In the Red Light District, Asa and Misty had learned each other better than before,

They talked, in-depth and, now as always, Asa Plenty the business man wanted more.

"My life, as of late, seems to have crumbled and will soon fall,

Before, I've been consumed by hate, so I'm so glad that you called.

Because I prayed, it must be God that let me open up my heart for you,

I was compelled by your integrity, after I left the cash and my card for you."

"I have prostate cancer, and time's leaving fast—this, I found out the other day,

By the sword I've caused so much pain to others with, I will die the same way.

In spite of all the money I've had, I was lacking as a man, mostly, as a father,

But meeting you has been a blessing from God; now, I can set my house in order."

"You see, denial's riddled me for a while, making me feel I am still a mack to the ladies,

Reality hit and I realized I'll die, so I prayed for the Lord to save me.

In a vision on my way to you, it came to me, to use my resources to start a foundation,

For wayward girls to start a new life, to repent and prevent my own damnation."

"Now, I need your help to champion my cause, your testimony will ensure that no man,

Is able to do, what's been done to you, to the girls that enter the program.

I've been guilty of what I aim to stop, to what you've been, often, subject to,

And, in you, I've found the perfect person, and I have found my program's director."

Misty burst into tears as she thought of the years, it'd been since feeling such gladness,

All she'd experienced, in her present state, had been a void left empty by sadness.

"Thank you, Mr. Plenty, for this chance; I can provide for my kids and, then,

Never will I have to be ashamed, worrying about judgment from parents of their friends."

He embraced her like a dad, "No need for thanks, you're helping more than you know,

I'm helping your life to be better; now, you're helping me, eternally, to save my soul.

My gold-digging girl Kimmie is gonna leave me, when she realizes the money is gone,

But that matters to me not; this will be the foundation building my eternal home."

Misty looked Asa straight in the face, confused because they had not known one another,

Then, humbly, she asked of him, "How is it that I fit in your puzzle?"

"It is because the seeds you bore, are what link you to me,

The son I mentioned is Chief Sitting Still, so your seeds will bear the fruit of my tree."

He asked her to accompany him to breakfast, so they could further discuss the future,

Both emotional and excited, they aimed to ensure the program was a true producer.

He said, "Let the redeemed say so with a joyful heart, and newly constructed views."

She added, "Thank the Lord it's out with the bad olds, and in us—the good news."

The News II: Testify

The Call to Worship

"Guide me, o thou, great Jehovah, pilgrim through this barren land,"

Deacon Upright, raising his hymn, sang stretching forth his work-hardened hands.

He proceeded to kneel next to a pew, praying and praising in devotion, he wept, too,

Enjoying one of the few traditions, that the growing church had kept to.

Since the new pastor had come, things had begun to happen, fast,

Service they had, in the new facility, wasn't like the prayer warriors of the past.

Wooden chairs with wicker backs, were replaced with fine ones fit for dining,

Ivory keys on a synthesizing keyboard, had replaced the sounds of old organs crying.

And in his church's rise, the pastor had had no reservations,

Saying he planned for a new age, and so catered to the younger generation.

Attendance multiplied in young adults, so had efforts not been for nothing,

Many elderly members had grown sick and tired, while many of them were shut in.

The positions that some people held, were not based on strength of their faith,

Rather how many degrees they'd received, and the state of affairs and their estates.

For years, the church had been a community pillar, for all, a beacon of hope,

During Civil Rights, they had had freedom schools, to help folks become able to vote.

They had done food drives on Thanksgiving, gathered toys for kids on Christmas,

Doing all within their power, to ensure no one felt like a misfit.

I've got my weekly church in, but I have had about enough,

I'm getting a little hungry, so I wish they would hurry up.

The way I have it figured, when Pastor goes up there to preach,

I'll catch the spirit, and he'll sit down, then, we can go and eat.

Hopefully, we will get out of here, in just a little while,

So I can call the girls, and talk about this scandal, child.

I am Sister Tellit, been tellin' it like it T-I is, since God put me here,

This church has always been my home; I've been head usher for forty years.

Look, there's cleavage you could cut, plenty of bosoms on display,

Lady Minister is a pushover, and the new choir director is gay.

Not that the pastor needs her help, he has true God-given ability,

Plus, the church would go to the dogs, if Lady Minister had too much responsibility.

Some folks used to call my grand pappy sexist, 'cause he was stubborn as a mule, when,

He knew what he was doing, keeping the role of women out of the pulpit.

With all of this foolishness, the good years we've had will, soon, be ending,

If it weren't for our good pastor, I can't say I would be attending.

People act like I'm the only one, who sees this business, in here,

Today, I only stay, 'cause it's Women's Day, and the church is serving dinner.

The matrons cherish the pastor but, amongst themselves, they want to fight,

It's always a mess, when you look to the left and strife, when you look to the right.

I can understand the fact, that we should take care of Pastor,

Plus, he teaches that The Word says if we don't, we are headed for disaster.

Just then, she was interrupted in her thinking and, also, forced to come to,

When, new member, Kimmie Samoa, needed to be excused into the pew.

"Hey, precious, how you doing," *she said as Kimmie proceeded sitting,*

"As always, young lady, you know that you sure look pretty."

Now, see, that's what I'm saying, Kimmie is an outstanding young lady,

She's young and educated, loves the Lord, and doesn't have a house full of babies.

She has not been here, very long—she's a newcomer to the city,

But she has been a blessing, working on our finance committee.

As Sister Tellit finished her thoughts, and offered Kimmie some stick peppermint,

The church ripped into hand claps, while Pastor de Cash approached the pulpit.

Seeing him as the future of the church, and hearing his voice of that of the Lord,

Sister Tellit did not hesitate, or attempt to hide her strong applause.

Like the kings of old, he energized the people with his very presence,

His charm shone through, even before he spoke—charisma made him luminescent.

The aura that surrounded him, had the people going wild and getting loud,

He could've been mistaken for their god, as he raised his hands to calm the crowd.

"I just love our pastor," *Sister Tellit said*, "He is so very good,"

Kimmie Samoa just nodded her head, acknowledging she agreed and understood.

On the edges of their seats, the congregation waited to hear from the,

Man who, moments earlier, mouthed the words "Thank You" to show humility.

"Today, service will be shorter, saints; at three o'clock, Women's Day will be beginning,

So, to make it all work, morning service will, soon, be ending.

I pray the Holy Spirit's sweet communion, will be on you and yours,

Please keep the sick and shut-in close to heart, and be benevolent with the poor."

"The way that we will do this, is the choir will come for service in song,

We will, then, bring His tithes and our offerings, and stay moving right along.

After we've opened up our pocketbooks, we'll prepare to open our hearts,

Lady Minister will come for altar prayer, then, I'll deliver the word of God."

Pastor de Cash sipped his orange juice—to keep his mouth from drying out,

Kimmie was startled by a woman, in front, rocking fast in her seat and crying out.

She thought, I get sick of looking at these "churchy" folks; they really are a trip,

Like the one they call Moms Aprayin'—she knows she really needs to quit.

Always screamin' and shoutin', steadily whining and wailing,

Anybody that sees her every Sunday, ought to know that she's just playing.

When it's time to do the offering, she won't put in a single dollar,

But she came in, this morning, before we've even started, she's ready to holler.

I bet if you were to ask her, she couldn't tell you who Moses was,

But not a single Sunday, will she let church start before she does.

And this fat thang sitting beside me, she stays up in my face,

Always smiling wide-eyed and admiring, like she does her dinner plate.

I already know I'm pretty, so that's something she doesn't have to tell,

And her nephews could graduate from Yale, and still wouldn't have a chance, in hell.

To religion, I'm not convinced; from here, I hope I'll, soon, be gone,

It's going to take a miracle, for God to show me He wants me for His own.

My father's name is Phil Myhand, he always "laid up his treasures in Heaven,"

Meanwhile, he's broke as a joke on Earth, and seems, always, to be settling.

I watched my mama support my dad, break his back to be a "righteous brother,"

For what, peanuts and scraps of kings—the working man really is a sucker.

My pray day is my pay day; it has to pay me dividends,

All that praisin' and prayin' my daddy did, and what did it ever get for him?

On the bottom, I never saw the top—knew nothing in between,

So broke, we fussed and, often, fought, over the pork in the pork 'n beans.

He always had a poor man's promise, full of advice and a head filled with dreams,

The best thing that came from years in the mill, was being fired when I turned eighteen.

I knew that once he'd lost his job, things would go from bad to worse,

I grabbed cash I'd made working in the mall—didn't look back after grabbing my purse.

I found a rich man about my father's age, he always showered me with the nicest,

Bags and gifts and exotic trips, until he had a midlife crisis.

He spoiled me something crazy, for the best part of a year,

I spent money at my leisure, with no limits or rules to which I had to adhere.

When all was gravy through my eyes, he said he had got a calling from above,

To use his funds to make a change, for girls substituting sex for love.

Yeah, whatever, I thought it was clever; he made an excuse out of women,

Instead of being honest, and admitting he was cutting off my spending.

I decided to leave the city and let him have his Lordy story,

Then, I refocused my attention, on finding a man who could afford me.

The choir had done one number, for their next, the music had begun to play,

The sound of Moms Aprayin' shouting and witnessing, woke Kimmie from her daze,

They wonder why I always cry; I can sense and hear them laughing,

But I'm praying for deliverance, claiming victory before it happens.

Israel Life always made my life complete—he gave my heart so much joy,

I thanked the Lord, daily, for such a bless-ed baby boy.

He is my child of promise; I had prayed that God would lift my gloom,

Three miscarriages, before I had my son, made me think I had a barren womb.

Israel's father died in the line of duty, shot by a bank robber, so I buried him,

Never getting to meet our son, his father passed away during the time I carried him.

Israel ever was so clever; there was nothing that could stump him,

Headstrong and stubborn, as a bull, he would always find a way to get what he wanted.

My baby was a schoolyard scholar, a young Christian and southern gent,

People admired his grooming—complimented his raising everywhere he went.

He always said "Mother may I," and never chose to disobey,

Never chose to skip homework or chores, before going outside to play.

When Israel Life was thirteen, he played basketball like he was always doing,

And in the shortest instant, his cousin was killed dead in a drive-by shooting.

They were more like brothers, since the tender age of two; they'd always been friends,

So Israel went and jumped into a gang, so they could help him go and get his revenge.

They never found the trigger man, so Israel's initiation had been for naught,

And as the months and years rolled by, his affiliation had become too deep to stop.

He kept some of the latest hours—he had grown to become so disrespectful,

Not to mention, his church attendance had gone to next to never.

All the drinking and partying, always hanging on the corner,

He was expelled from high school, when they caught him possessing marijuana.

People talk, so I paid no mind, when they said he was a geeker,

The last straw was when he pawned my watch—I heard he sold groceries out my freezer.

He is my only child so, for my attention, he had no rival,

Could it be I loved Israel Life so much, that I made him into an idol?

I did my best with that boy; my Lord has to know I tried,

Maybe, I began to worship him, and so God let him make me cry.

I know my son is in the streets, and we aren't, now, the way we were,

His body has become a slave, to a local dealer known as Pharaoh Sir.

These trying times, in my life, have made me study the word more,

So, like in Exodus, that Pharaoh's gonna have to let my Israel go.

Until it happens, I will believe, that God will bring me peace,

Steadily, I will be on my knees—bleeding him in the blood of Jesus.

I know my God will bring him home, and give him a way to wake up,

If only to reward the faith I've had, like Abraham, Isaac, and Jacob.

The choir seemed to be on fire, but there had been a dull moment with them, never,

In the time that they'd been under the direction of Leo Todd, their new young director.

He seemed soft-spoken, and so timid even feminine,

And was regarded as being funny, because of his little contact with women in.

The congregation in which he praised, and the choir that he directed,

Women insinuated, all the time; their approaches, he just rejected.

He put his all into spirit stirring—was, in no way, in between,

Always adding jazzy pizzazz, when he taps the tambourine.

But even in the midst of his praise, he couldn't help but hear people down him,

So he developed strong contempt, for those who attended and were around him.

They snicker, each time I turn my back, speculating that I must be gay,

But I was sent here on a mission, so there's a role that I must play.

Instead of just having the decency, to ask about my sexual orientation,

They'd rather get in circles and talk, starting a buzz in the congregation.

Since I know the truth, it doesn't bother me or really make a difference,

They are just, constantly, proving, how much church folks differ from Christians.

I should turn my frown around, and put a smile upon my face,

'Cause, in just a little while, I can, for good, rid myself of this place.

Regardless to what the congregation said, he took it in stride and stayed to himself,

In fact, there were few he would talk to, and only one he would go to for help.

That was his choir's gem Jessie Bell, who he knew could always bring life to the room,

With her notes and regal voice—he was glad, because her solo would come, soon.

As Jessie Bell came to the mic, her favorite "Precious Lord," she wanted to render,

She caught Sister Tellit's attention, with usual thoughts of judgment and her opinion.

Look at ol' Jessie Bell, that there is a tricky thang,

I'll give credit where credit is due; she can open up her mouth and sang.

She sings, each week, lifting praise, with her voice so strong and husky,

Knowing good and well, she ain't never been nothing but a hussy.

She came and rejoined the church, one day, and has sang here, ever since,

I believe God can change us all but, with her, I'm not convinced.

She was, always, fast and Omish—the type that's known for going to park,

If a boy's shoes would shine in the light, he could have her in the dark.

She and I went to school, together, I've known her all of our lives,

From first grade all the way through—graduated in the class of sixty-five.

My daddy told me, as far as us being friends, I had better find another,

'Cause all fast gals do is lie, and find ways to stir up trouble.

It's a wonder she even has a voice, or at least one that can be useful,

Lord knows, she smoked seems like forever and, for years, she was a boozer.

She sang at all the juke joints, did every request the crowd would want,

Always, she was a favorite, at after-hours honky tonks.

She was blessed with a body, since before I can remember,

Her features were delicate but well-developed—blossoming bosom young and tender.

Black pumps seemed to make her glide; her shirts had fit her form like they were tailored,

The split of her mini-skirts, almost met the split that the good Lord gave her.

Because she started fast, so young, she had shown the signs of time,

I say since we graduated in sixty-five, she was farted out by sixty-nine.

Silky soul singer, she bumped and grinded around the floor,

Sometimes, it took a hit of liquor, most times, she was a natural whore.

No matter what the case, despite how Sister Tellit had chose to put it,

Jessie Bell seemed to have the Holy Spirit on her, and she knew just how to move it.

She rose with the choir behind her, everyone on one accord,

She was beautifully brilliant, raising her voice unto the Lord.

It seemed as though to rejoice His grace, would be the only way to please her,

With a voice so strong and rich, she did sound every bit like Shirley Caesar.

Sweeping the congregation, she sang with intensity and fire,

And stirred the Holy Spirit, by sending up timbrel and lyre.

Deacons clapped and tapped their fee;, matrons waved their hands, as they walked,

The ushers called for backup fans; the nurse's guild needed more smelling salts.

The Holy Spirit, truly, had its way; His lamb could have praised for days,

This was the strongest faith display, at the church, in this present age.

The thunder began to boom, outside, like cymbals crashing and thudding,

Out of nowhere, it had come; the storm began all of a sudden.

Tears streamed, as she sang, thoughts of her past came back and across her,

Mind as she thought of God's goodness—through all the things that He brought her.

My life has been a roller coaster; I've seen its highs and lows,

From singing about God's goodness, to shaking and gyrating my hips at smoky shows.

I've heard the preacher say, "God takes care of children and fools,"

I am living proof, that both of these are true.

When I was a girl of twelve, I began to get a fat backside and stacked,

Once puberty began to hit me, it rared back with a baseball bat.

I paid it no attention, my body made no difference to me, at all,

I was just a choir kid, no interest in boys—just playing with dolls.

There was a deacon, at the church—he had been nothing but nice to me, never,

He was like a brother to my father, in fact, I used to call him uncle Mo Lester.

In those days, the deacon board met on evenings the choir had to practice,

To save money on the light bill because, honestly, we just didn't have it.

Mo Lester offered to drive me home, in his fifty-seven Chevrolet,

He said it was getting dark, and he wanted to be sure that I'd get home safe.

As he drove the long way home, he began to go under my dress with his hand,

I resisted but he persisted—said he wanted me to know how to pleasure a man.

That night was a first, but many would follow, in similar fashion,

With me catering to his requests, anything sexual that he could imagine.

He convinced me he was my teacher, and that I really did need him,

I never knew I was being molested, because I had really believed him.

So as I grew, I embraced my sex life and body with no "buts,"

I knew I could pleasure boys my age, since I was able to please a grown-up.

When I realized what was happening, I can't say it didn't hurt,

But I couldn't say anything, because Mo Lester's family was royalty in our church.

His father was the founding pastor; his daughter Sister Tellit still governs the ushers,

But the family, still, serves two masters, his grandson Pharaoh Sir is a local crack hustler.

Mo made me turn, heavily, to drinking, as I'd begun becoming grown,

I searched for love, in men, that I had lost respect for at home.

I had lost respect for my daddy; my hatred grew so strong, you wouldn't believe,

To the years of my molesting, how could he have been so naïve?

The innocence that was taken from me, could not be given by another,

And it hurt my heart to know, that my father had called him "brother."

I held hate so close to heart; my father's love was what I fought,

Even though I never told it, so I thought what I got was all my fault.

From a middle class upbringing, I guess that that just goes to show,

The underside can be happening to any class of folks, all along, and no one knows.

Regardless of the situation, my letter had been made scarlet,

And I was just regarded, as being a little harlot.

Once I had made up in my mind, that I would go and make amends,

I was too late to make it right; Daddy died, before I came, amongst family and friends.

After years of searching, for new men to be my daddy,

God showed me He had never left—that He had always had me.

My hope is people will hear me sing, and not credit me for making them shake or shiver,

Just know that I've been a broken fool and, for them, too, He'll be a deliverer.

As the choir and musicians continued to sing and play, lifting praise up to the sky,

The congregation stood up for the offering, waiting to come around the church's sides.

Contempt was in Kimmie's glance; Moms Aprayin' nodded cordially, just the same,

The look on Kimmie's face, was one indicating, "Now, that's a shame."

The older lady tried to pay it no mind, she just readied all the money she had to give,

Her only offering was a dollar, but she made sure it was as neat as possible and crisp.

I used to be an English teacher, helping students meet basic requirements,

But had a breakdown when Israel broke my heart, and I had to take early retirement.

I was a cheerful giver—to those in need, I was always kind,

But, now, I'm on fixed income, so I mostly tithe with my time.

People about material things, look at me funny when my tithe envelope is missing,

But I think helping folks get their GED, is one way of helping to feed God's children.

My wisdom is not that of God's, so I do not claim to know what He knows,

If I start to think my life is hard, I just look at the love He showed to Job.

I don't have much money, now, but all of my needs are still met,

Like Elijah, by the brook Cherith, I always have my daily bread.

There will be a day of deliverance, and I know it will come in time,

I could have lost every lick of sense, but I thank God that He let me keep my mind.

The Invitation

"Lady Minister did, now, as always, before any step she made or trod,

Whispering a prayer of submission and surrender, humbling herself before her God.

She opened herself, completely, to be ready for the Lord to speak to her,

Asking her own decrease so He could increase, and His spirit could work through her.

To the decision-making process, the pastor kept her absent for two years being there,

And her only responsibility had been to lead the church in prayer.

She had never thought small of her simple duties, with faith that never did falter,

Taking account that all is done, for the perfect will of her heavenly father.

And so she approached the pulpit, nothing out of the usual, on that day,

It's a blessing she expected, Him to use her in a mighty way.

With a voice so noble, not disturbed by cracks or squeaks,

And nothing in mind but a charge to keep, Lady Minister began to speak.

"Now, we will have our altar call, you can come forth or remain standing,

What's important is you bring your burdens forth, and that you, then, unhand them.

All of you are welcome to come to the front, or stay right where you are,

Our God could hear the cries of your heart, in crowded rooms or silence in your cars."

"In a moment, we will hear God's word, and it'll be obeying time,

But, now, if all hearts and minds are clear, children of God, it's prayin' time.

Father God, who art in Heaven, we haven't come here for a show,

But to see You fulfill Your bless-ed will; You are the greatest love we know."

"You are a healer and deliverer, a doctor and a comforter,

You are the king of kings, who has made us more than conquerors.

Your wisdom is so infinite, it cannot be imagined,

Your power is a mighty miracle; mercy is from everlasting to everlasting."

"You are the I Am of the burning bush—Lily of the Valley, oh Lord, You are Him,

The hand that led father Abraham, You are the Morning Star that will never dim.

You are the one, who made the seas to calm, or the rocks to cry out loud,

You are the merciful judge that gave law to Moses with lightning from the cloud."

The congregation witnessed to the preacher, shouting and clapping, within the pews,

Hollers resounded "Lord have mercy," the Holy Spirit had continued to move.

Speaking in tongues, people moaned hymns; oh, the spirit remained high, it,

Was like the Pentecost, as true believers praised in their native language.

Of course, no man could understand the plan, but it was evident that God was in it,

All looked on with hope, as if expecting a miracle any minute.

Lady Minister had just called upon the Lord, already, a church service hard to forget,

And she hadn't even told mountains to move—hadn't petitioned to the father, yet.

"Lord, all of us, right now, are standing in the need of blessing,

Some have pain, while some have strain, but we all need a heaping Heaven helping.

We know You know our hearts, oh Lord, even if, our needs, we haven't mouthed them,

And faith leads us to know, whatever it is, You can bring us up and out it."

"I don't know everybody's trouble, but I know You can make them right,

Our just Lord and Savior, please hear saints' and sinners' cries, alike.

Reach beyond the prison walls; give the homeless somewhere to lay their heads,

Lead the lame to stand and walk; give the hungry stomach its daily bread."

"There's someone in our midst, oh Lord, who's praying their child will come home,

Please take that child's hand and guide, let them leave the drugs alone.

Bless us in a mighty way, like Your love, let Your blessings never stop,

Strengthen us as Your body, as we try to lead sheep to Your flock."

The presence of the Lord was clear, as service became highly spiritual,

And the faith of the congregation could've, itself, produced a miracle.

There was a lot of praise—Lady Minister continued her petition before the Lord,

While the musician made the keyboard speak, with melodies and chords.

Just then, the vestibule doors swung open, and a man began to enter,

His matted hair was uncombed and kept, a bearded face like you'd expect in winter.

In with him, came the strongest scent of beer and cigarettes,

The light, shining behind him, left him as only a silhouette.

Though he seemed so out of place, his forward focus wouldn't falter,

As if he had a made up mind, and wouldn't stop until he reached the altar.

The veins of his tattooed arms, were bulging through his skin,

Track marks looked like stories in Braille, scattered along and throughout the bends.

He approached the altar, at the front, as tears trickled his cheeks,

As old members recognized him, their clapping, quickly, turned to loss of speech.

Someone who resembles him, a coincidence, could it be,

They looked again just to be sure, was it really he?

"I wish this had been easier for me, I wish this would have been simpler,

Seven times, I've walked around this church, trying to make a decision to enter.

I thought of all the wrong things I've done—the things that I've been through,

And knew not if the door was open to me, thought my welcome was worn out, here, too."

"I've made a lot of mistakes, in life, improper turns down the road I've gone,

But even in my sinful soul, I still know what's right from wrong.

I hope that God will cleanse my soul, relieve the burden of all my sinning,

I want to be taken back to the water but, first, I have come, today, to be a witness."

"I am ashamed to say, but the truth is as plain as this,

I was gonna burglarize the church, and take what I found to get a fix.

I had cased the church for a couple of days, until well over into the night,

Timing when people left for the evening, even knew the times they turned off the lights."

"I'd remember who would go and come, and clocked all the times they'd meet,

And nothing looked suspicious, because I scored dope at a house just down the street.

No one ever recognized my face; to them, I must've been a packet-toting flunkie,

Or because of my dress, some probably just said, "Lord, have mercy on that junkie."

"I finally had a made-up mind, I had planned my work so didn't have a need to worry,

The time to act had, quickly, come; I would move after midweek bible study.

I eased through dimly-lit spots, weaved through trees and hid behind trucks,

In case I had to run and, then, got pinched, no one could pick me from a lineup."

"Once I got up to the church, I was startled to see a sight,

It was the pastor's car that was parked, conveniently, away from any kind of streetlight.

I saw that no one was in it, and figured that maybe he'd left with a deacon,

To visit the sick and shut-in, or someone else who needed prayer or seeing."

"I snuck around to the finance room; my research said that that was my way in,

There was a lock on the window, but it was old and the lock had a bend.

I had a screwdriver to jimmy the lock with like, at many a house, I had done,

Just then, as I peeked in, a light from a lamp on the desk flashed on."

"I thought, as I looked on, at first, the preacher must be really dedicated,

To be in the church house, so late, but I saw, better, after I waited.

The more and more I looked at it, the more I thought it might be fishy,

And I knew they weren't just friendly from church, when I saw them getting frisky."

"I was shocked to see the beloved pastor was, in the dark, really living grimy,

He kissed his vixen with an open mouth, and couldn't stop grabbing on her heiny.

Make no mistake about it, saints; I knew exactly what I was seeing,

They weren't having church, but they were definitely touching and agreeing."

"They took money from the combination safe, while I still hid and looked,

They wrote checks to phantom companies, so it would balance out the books."

If you call the last six businesses, that are listed on the list,

Don't be surprised if, by chance, you find a dial tone, because they do not exist."

The preacher had tried to stay calm, he had done all he could to stay resistant,

To anger, but was losing the battle with forsaking wrath, he was becoming indignant.

"Are you really gonna believe this trash; this young man's wasting the church's time,

Not only is devil's poison running through his veins, but his lies occupy his mind."

"Pastor, you can say whatever you like, and take whatever jabs at me,

I know I'm not a perfect man, and I've never claimed to be.

I've prayed about all the wrong I've done, and know God will forgive even this,

But you are the worst kind of man—you are a hypocrite."

The pastor continued to deny Israel, quickly, he had tried to dismiss him,

Israel looked over the crowd, and pointed to Kimmie Samoa as who he'd seen kissing.

"You just shut your mouth, crackhead, *"Kimmie Samoa said, wiping her eyes,*

"Sure, I helped him embezzle, but I only did it, twice."

Just then, Leo Todd stepped from the choir stand, pulling a walkie talkie from his belt,

Into it, he said to get in place, as he approached Pastor de Cash on the pastor's left.

His whole demeanor seemed to change; he became firm not with flamboyant sinew,

And with a look of interest in his face, he urged Israel to "Please, continue."

"You can shut it, too, Leo, just worry about your choir stand,

Shouldn't you be doing something, like secretly watching somebody's man?"

With insistent reassurance, Leo placed his hand upon the pastor's shoulder,

And as Kimmie finished insinuating, straight-faced speaking, this is what he told her:

"Well, see that's where you're wrong, Miss, my wife never wants for a single thing,

It's just she's not here with me, because I've been on a six month sting.

I've heard all the whispering and gossip that church folks, often, tend to do,

I came here just to get the pastor but, now, I have gotten you, too."

"He had fooled other congregations, saying any problem he could solve it,

Then, they bought him expensive homes, which he sold to pocket the profit.

He's been a belly-slivering snake, too smooth to be caught in his web of lies,

We'd either have to catch him cold, or find a single witness who could testify."

"Our service is recorded for broadcast, so you've just confessed on tape,

So, to avoid a hefty sentence, too, I suggest that you turn state.

Evidence against this miscreant, no need for both of you to take a fall,

We've been on him for quite some time, now, the Feds are gonna nail him to the wall."

She'd had no intention of stewardship, to church participation, she'd been a no show,

But to hear Kimmie begin to sing, you would think she had a solo.

"I've lived the po' folks plight in life, what a drab, you can have it,

So when I saw the luxury I could laugh in, I had to jump down and grab it."

"The internet's such a useful tool, and not just for lonely hearts and cougars,

I got on the social networks, to look through prospective suitors.

Dope boys I'd known in high school, had long since tried to get with this,

But I thought out to myself, the reward did not match the risk."

"The way that luck would have it, I had stumbled on a lick,

If I played it right, I stood a good chance to get rich, quick.

He spoke about the way to play it—the risk and, too, the rules,

When you speak of gettin' money, it always gets me in the mood."

"Even the smallest detail, he could not afford to negate,

Said he pastors at a church, somewhere, so he partied out of state.

He said he wanted me to join his church, and it'd only be a matter of time,

Before I'd be in the finance room, and we could rob those suckers, blind."

"I used to watch my daddy praise, and wonder what's the use,

In praying to a God that you can't see, to help you just to get through.

All that churching, singing in choirs—serving on usher boards,

But all I felt each time I prayed, was that of reciting words."

"I would approach him, as he kneeled, eyes so wet and red he couldn't see,

Each time I asked what he prayed for, he'd say he prayed for me.

'But Daddy, I'm okay,' I'd say, with crying, I had hoped he'd be through,

'I know you are, okay, today,' he'd say, 'but I'm praying He will keep you."

"I've dreamed for what seems like my whole life, wanting money for things I could get,

But it wasn't until this very moment, that it makes sense and I see that I am rich.

God gave me a role to play at church, when I had none left anywhere else,

So as far as the courtroom, I'll go testify, if I have to go by myself."

Just as Leo was getting what he needed, a firsthand testimony and mountain of proof,

The spirit of the living God got hold of Moms Aprayin', and would not turn her loose.

"Lord, thank You for revealing this wolf, taking advantage of Your sheep,

In one blessing, You've given our church a miracle, and returned my prodigal son to me."

Leo Todd said, "Lady Minister, you're in charge, now, from what I can see or I can tell,

'Cause this bottom-feeding scavenger's mine, and he has a reservation at the jail."

With the pastor caught and cuffed, Leo walked him out with a smile he couldn't hide,

And Lady Minister wasted no time, going to Kimmie Samoa's confessing side.

"Folks will indulge in the devil's decadence, shameless to pleasures he affords,

But you've done what church folks fail to do, you're testifying for the Lord.

Though Satan has had you seduced, to his shiny lifestyle, you've been a slave,

If you believe in your heart, right now, my child, then, right now, you have been saved."

Crying, Kimmie replied, "I need to apologize to my daddy, for how he must view me,

And tell him that I have found the Lord, and let Daddy see the new me."

Lady Minister said, "If it's all the same, we hope God moves you to stay and help us out,

Call your daddy and tell him the good news, but you're already in your Father's house."

Sister Tellit had held her peace for far too long, and she could not continue to sit,

"Oh, no; she has got to go—my family has done too much in here for me to tolerate this."

Lady Minister was ready to respond; she had God's wisdom but had been kept quiet,

But, now, she could say what God laid on her heart, and would not let anybody deny it.

"There's no time constraints on His will, though we don't know what is to come,

Look how long our journeys took, and just look what the Lord has done.

We have witnessed a miracle, in front of our very eyes when,

We came to church to worship, who knew we would have a revival?"

"Time has to play out, so loose ends can be fastened,

If our pasts hadn't been, then, the present couldn't happen.

Today's example reminds me of what I've read, and it goes as such,

God asked Job why he spoke so much, when he didn't know enough."

"If I stood on my front porch, and threw a rock in a pack of dogs, they would all look,

And you can bet your bottom dollar, that the hit dog of them would holler.

Believe this when I tell you and, please, make no doubt about it,

If what's being said hits close to home, you'll feel conviction and think about it."

"Though you weren't in the finance room, stealing tithes or having sex,

Think before you judge, because no sin outweighs the next.

If you plan to stone a wretch, for the times when they were blind, then,

You had better say your peace, and go to take your place beside them."

"Idolatry and gluttony, pride and sloth are just as bad as lust,

No matter what temptation, flesh is the original sin and the fall of all of us.

We're quick to point a stiffened finger, wanting the "cancer" removed, pronto,

Neglecting that it is, often, we who are the ones that made the monster."

"I see a lot of people feeling, that their mistakes make God refuse them,

Like some old choices that they've made, make Him less able to use them.

This makes for such grief-filled groans; it helps see to it that hope is lessened,

Future blessings can never come to be, 'cause past struggles hinder minds in the present."

"Things can escape from human understanding; we don't see things the way God sees,

He can take the scraps of a man, and make, from them, a masterpiece.

Abram would stretch the truth; Moses took away a life,

Noah drank a little; David sent a man to battle in order to have his wife."

"Each day I live, I am a little closer to the table that's already been set,

And I'm so glad to say, with a smile on my face, God's not through with us, yet.

Let it marinate for a minute, and it'll make sense to you, too,

That every saint has a past, while every sinner has a future."

"Realize what you've seen in your past, things you've had to deal with,

May be medicine for those going through it, now—something that they can heal with.

Take this pain to cleanse your heart, and be a salve to your soul,

Let confronting your past bring you comfort—forgiveness to make you whole."

"Instead of being Christ's body, touching others so His spirit can move through them,

We, more times than not, preach at and talk down to them.

So, my brothers and sisters, I say to you, don't be so holy you have to hide,

Right where you are, raise your hands to the sky—take the stand and testify."

Immediately, Jessie Bell waved her hand; the spirit was on her and getting stronger,

She had bore the burden of a life of pain, and refused to bear it any longer.

"You are so right, Lady Minister; I've had pain, most of my life, that I've let fester,

When I was twelve, I began being hurt, by the respected deacon, Mr. Mo Lester."

"He made a personal sex toy of me—he used me and abused me,

His good name stayed intact, while he helped ridicule me as a floozy.

His inner sins helped to rob me of my innocence—his growth helped mine to cease,

My oils that were once extra virgin were, now, used up and no more than dirty grease."

"All throughout my high school years, the town looked at me like I was so bad,

Little did they know, I had been exploited by a close friend of my dad.

Then, I found the only man, that I felt had ever loved me,

He accepted me with flaws and all—never took ample chances to judge me."

"You could find Percy the Pincher big-eyed and smiling, a pinch of 'bacco in his cheek,

Never too caught up in signifying, to tip his hat to ladies in order to speak.

Gentle with women and children, he took no opportunity to be mean,

And what a personality—as close to perfect that I have seen."

"His grandma had raised him best she knew, with God's help, she raised him right,

But some folks looked down on him, 'cause he could hardly read or write.

He was such a tender heart, never mistaken for inconsiderate,

Well educated from the streets, the "sophisticated" still just called him illiterate."

"So polite and in tune with deference, his very presence was a blessing,

His life was such a courtesy lesson; you couldn't help but to respect him.

He believed in death before dishonor, never backed down from a fight,

Some say he had a death wish, I say he was passionate for what is right."

"Not just a common hoodlum, but he was far away from boring,

Coming along before his time, he was like a grandpa the way he told a story.

He told me of one time, in particular, and it has always stayed in my head,

I can still hear his words so clear, and this is what he said:"

"Maybe I haven't led a spotless life, a life that's white and pure,

But if the Klan had caught me ridin' home, that night, they'd string me up, for sure.

I know I shoulda took advice, when folks said I was a fool,

Runnin' 'round from church to church, talkin' bout a freedom school."

"Now, I'm runnin' for my life, tryin' best to stay out their way,

Turnin' up and down all those dusty roads, in my muddy Chevrolet.

Duckin' and dodgin' and hittin' the lights, just so my tag wouldn't show,

Sneakin' 'round like a thief in the night, through every crook and turn that I knowed."

"Pastor had just preached 'bout the last gonna be first, like he said in our Bible study,

Just hope I got home 'fore the Klan spot me out, wanted my head beat red and bloody.

Said a pickup came through, last week; the men was drunk, had bottles and bats,

Told folks that was there they ain't mean them no harm, just askin bout where'n I'm at."

"I ain't no fool, I know what they wanted, if happened they come findin' me,

They was gonna want, since I'm fightin' for freedom, to see me swingin' from a tree.

Oh Lord what was that, it was some lights in the mirror, and look like they was a'comin,'

Took my mind off gettin' home, away from the Klan, had it on a hymn I was hummin."

"I had to speed up, if they caught me, they'd kill me fa' sho,'

Wasn't gonna be able to be seein' my mama no mo.'

So I whispered a little prayer and said 'Protect me, my father,'

Then, I whipped 'round the bend and mashed the gas even harder."

"They was bumpin' my bumper and they was ridin' me heavy,

But that ol' pickup truck just couldn't ride like my Chevy.

Anything they could do, I knowed they was gonna try me,

Then, I thought hit the brakes, and let 'em blow right on by me."

"So I cut off my lights, and duck off fast as I can,

Thank God I knew those ol' roads, like it was the back of my hand.

They turned around to look for me, like huntin' dogs in the night,

And I watched that ol' truck, 'til it went clean outta sight."

"I turned my lights on, and propped a stick to the gas,

And ran the other way, what other choice did I have?

I ran as fast as I could, until I almost threw up,

Heard a boom and saw flames, car must've hit a tree and blew up."

"I guess the Klan must've thought, I got burned up in the flames,

I hid under a nearby porch, and stayed there 'til mornin' came.

I worked even harder, to get the Word to the people,

Couldn't nobody tell me, God wouldn't deliver us from evil."

As she continued, Jessie Bell's eyes went from partly cloudy to heavy downpour,

Momentarily, she'd stop when she got full, then, she'd say a little more.

Anyone with eyes could see, she was no stranger to the rain,

First, she talked with pride of her love, now, it was transformed into pain.

"I had never doubted his bravery, never one to boast but showed it more than most,

Then, I was blessed and cursed, to have to see it all, up close.

After he'd escaped from them, the beef with him would only strengthen and grow bigger,

They had been put to shame, when outsmarted by what they called that "ignorant nigger.""

"Percy had almost died fighting for freedom—protection, how could anyone deny him,

Shop owners and the poor folks he worked for, did what they had to do to try to hide him.

The clerks at the corner grocery, made sure he had bread and meat to eat,

And the people at the pool hall, prepared the back room for him to sleep."

"Bringing tears to my eyes during a sneak visit, he said it was my husband he chose to be,

Sharking at the pool hall and knocking hustles, he'd bought a ring to propose to me.

He placed the ring on my finger, while I couldn't stop the rolling tears,

We made up our minds to leave, soon, openly fantasizing about how we'd live."

"I pleaded with him to make love to me, I begged him for sexing,

Because my body had always been my value—my only way to show affection.

Then, he kissed me on my forehead, as he walked me to the door,

Remaining too much of a gentleman, to let me stay and celebrate engagement more."

"No windows on the door, had made it possible for him to hide,

So there was no way of knowing, what fate awaited on the other side.

There was a group of white boys, with crow bars and baseball bats, in hand,

Who had never been proven, but were rumored to run with the Klan."

"Tobacco juice splashed in puddles, the air smelt of cigarettes blazing,

Their truck's back glass was decorated by a rifle, and a rebel flag a-waiving.

The look on Percy's face, went from serenity to survival,

Recognizing the pickup from that dusty road, he knew it was time to pay the piper."

"They were all as drunk as skunks, all smelt of beer and shining stills,

Saying they heard that I was where they should come, to get they self a thrill.

They all seemed to find it funny, but Percy surely didn't,

And with each of their jive remarks, he grew more and more indignant."

"Thank God Percy had "mother wit," if he had nothin' else,

He realized if he planned to save my life, he would have to sacrifice himself.

When one of them reached to grab me, Percy gave little regard to his "place" or the law,

As fast as a streak of lightning, Percy sucker punched one of them square in his jaw."

"He yelled for me to run like hell, and fended them off so I could get away,

The last I ever saw of him, was another of them taking the butt of a rifle to his face.

They piled him into the truck's bed, tires screeching in the night as they held him down,

Word spread, two days later, his body was found in a creek castrated and drowned."

"Mo Lester could never take it, thinkin' I could love another man,

So when Percy's blood ran, it just as well landed on his hands.

If it weren't for your daddy's malice, from seein' Percy and me around the town, then,

He might still be alive, 'cause the Klan would have never found him."

"His want for what he wanted was clear to me, to others, it may have been deceiving,

Only he could've tipped them, because only he knew where I'd be for the evening."

Having tolerated as much of a tongue lashing, as she could stand in a single day,

Sister Tellit said, "Lord have mercy on your soul, for treating His children this way."

Jessie Bell had had enough of Sister Tellit, acting as if she had been offended,

Her reign of messiness had gone on far too long and, so, Jessie Bell planned to end it.

Because she stood in the sanctuary, she thought, perhaps, she shouldn't,

But she knew if she didn't speak out, there were too many others that wouldn't.

"You know you have some kind of nerve, hiding behind the salvation of the Son,

Just look at all the hearts you've hurt—at all of the low down that you have done.

Who ordained you as God's chosen, to determine the anointed or who should be blessed,

You've had a voice for far too long, and it's time I lay it to rest."

"If your grandfather's turning in his grave, it's because your family broke his heart with,

The poison you give the community he loved, and make malice in the church he started.

Your nephew makes sure dope gets sold, running Pyramid Homes with an iron fist,

Most residents can't afford a pot to piss, but find money to pay him for a fix."

"You've headed the ushers for forty years, been in this church for all of your life,

And, in that time, you've caused such strife, never have you provided light.

You've kept mess on right and left, claiming this one's scandalous, that one's a stripper,

Even said the new reverend is irrelevant, while passing notes or in hushed up whispers."

"That's right, you've never had a husband, or a man to have some children,

Too busy judging private lives in public, worrying about other people's business.

Never knowing when to speak—when to leave well enough alone,

Always keeping mess fresh on top, like is done with a butter churn."

"You've made men divorce their wives, because you swore she was a trollop,

Busy being a busy body, you have personified a gossip.

For someone with so much to say—a tongue that never keeps its discipline,

How is it Sister Tellit, you can crown yourself as the chief Christian?"

"You go wrong in thinking, church ends and starts inside these four walls,

Not taking into account daily ministry, or regular lives He touches and calls."

Gesturing to Israel, she said, "This young man's an admitted thief and in God's wisdom,

He laid His powerful hands on him, using him to help bring order to His kingdom."

"What's the matter, you look so surprised, I'm saying what you should already know,

Makes me wonder if you even read that bible, or just tote it around for show.

Well, know His will shall be done, in spite of and despite you,

I only hate that there are so many around the world, and they are just like you."

Marred by her hypocrisy, and overshadowed by her shame,

Sister Tellit turned so she could exit, out of the same door in which she came.

The incident ended not as she'd intended, all in attendance could see that that was fact,

She cried out as she hit the door, "I'm gone and won't be coming back!"

The remaining crowd testified and praised for hours, agreeing on vast decisions,

On how they would escape the talons of church folks, and get back to old time religion.

Compelled by the testimony of Jessie Bell, they vowed to start helping hurting women,

And Kimmie Samoa knew she could get help, by calling her old friend Asa Plenty.

When church dismissed after Christian bliss, Israel Life made his way outside,

And saw that the dreary clouds of storm, had parted in the sky.

"Look at the beautiful rainbow," *he said as he took it all in,*

"It's God's promise our storm is over, and will never come, again."

Dear Reader,

I would like to take this time to thank God for allowing me to present this to you and giving me the strength to do it. Though I penned the stories, there were a lot of people who helped make it possible. I don't want to begin to name names, because I don't want to exclude anyone that helped me realize my dream. However, I will say that I appreciate everything—from your prayers and support to your feedback on the unfinished manuscript. Thank you. I love you all—whoever and wherever you are. Also, I would like to take the opportunity to thank everyone for reading. I hope that something that was stated on the previous pages will be useful in your own individual walk of life. It is from the bottom of my heart that I wish you the best and hope that you have been as blessed reading these stories as I have been writing them. There will be more to come, if it's God's will, and nothing happens. If you need to contact me with questions, comments, or concerns, feel free to contact me at the following;

Friend me on Facebook: Hunter Johnson

Follow me on Twitter: @hunterjohnsonpresents

Email me: hunterjohnsonpresents@gmail.com

Visit me: www.hunterjohnson.net

www.ingramcontent.com/pod-product-compliance
Lightning Source LLC
Chambersburg PA
CBHW071834020426
42331CB00007B/1731